HANDBOOKS OF EUROPEAN NATIONAL DANCES

EDITED BY
VIOLET ALFORD

DANCES OF FRANCE

III: The Pyrenees

Plate 1   Vallée de Campan

DANCES of FRANCE
III: The Pyrenees

VIOLET ALFORD

NOVERRE PRESS

COLOUR ILLUSTRATIONS BY
G. DOUGLAS HALLIDAY
ASSISTANT EDITOR
YVONNE MOYSE

First published in 1952
This edition published in 2021 by
The Noverre Press
Southwold House
Isington Road
Binsted
Hampshire
GU34 4PH

ISBN 978-1-914311-1-27-7

© 2021 The Noverre Press

CONTENTS

INTRODUCTION	*Page* 7
French Catalonia	8
Dances Innumerable	9
Farandole and Contrapás	10
Carnival	10
The Bear Hunt	11
The Lez Valley and Balaguères	13
The Valley of Campan	14
Witches' Dances	14
The Basque Country	15
Music	17
Costume	19
When Dancing May Be Seen	21
Groups of Regional Dancers	22
THE DANCES	23
Poise of the Body and Holds	24
Basic Steps	24
Bail de la Courre	25
Encadenat	30
Bourrée Ariégeoise	32
La Castagne	34
Era Pelha ded Gat	36
BIBLIOGRAPHY	40

Illustrations in Colour, pages 2, 12, 29, 39
Map of the Pyrenees, page 6

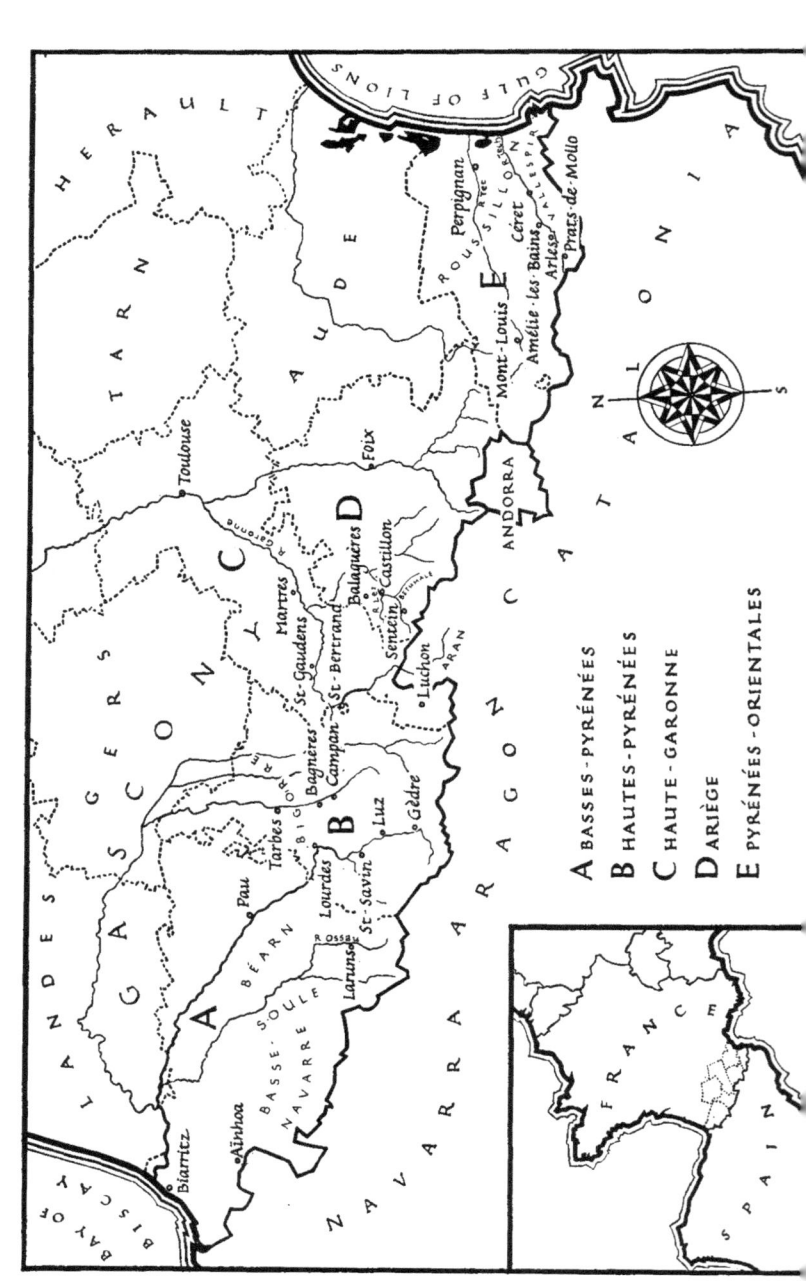

INTRODUCTION

In their climate, people and dances the Pyrenees may be divided into three regions. The eastern end of the range shows Mediterranean influence, the western, Atlantic; to the east the Spanish-Catalan style is seen in the dances and music, to the west, though dance and music are distinctly Basque (not French), they are in some degree influenced by Spanish-Basque traditions. But one thinks the central region could not possibly be coloured by influences from across the frontier, so high is the barrier, so inaccessible the peaks. Nevertheless one does find the same tradition of men's processional dances in single file in Aragon as in Bigorre on the French side, the same Pyrenean six-stringed drum, the same stick dances. There is in fact a Pyrenean type overruling regional types, and this applies to customs of nearly every sort.

In Andalusia woman shines in the dance, her partner a foil and background. As one goes north, man becomes more dominant, until in the Pyrenees he is predominant, the woman stepping low and discreetly, always following the steps set by her partner. It is not till we cross the Loire that equality is attained, as in the Breton dances.

Very interesting it is to note that classical ballet steps are the foundation of practically all men's dances. I have constantly seen pas battus, entrechats (superbly performed), grands battements, a high jeté en avant, pirouettes, cabrioles. In the Basque Carnival masquerade the processional is quite literally composed of the pas de basque. The question of how and when Pyrenean folk steps reached the ballet opens other questions which have not yet been answered.

FRENCH CATALONIA

The department called Pyrénées-Orientales was carved out of the old province of Roussillon which had belonged to Catalonia. It has been handed backwards and forwards between Spain and France by political treaties unconcerned with the human element involved. Customs, music, dance belong to Catalan culture. Catalan Cobla bands, full of life and noise, still mark every fête, though the little *flaviol* and tiny wrist-drum, so like our English pipe and tabor, have dropped out on the French side of the frontier. To make up for this loss the Spanish-Catalan Sardana has arrived, over the mountains as well as up the coast, for it is passionately danced in high Vallespir, *Vallis Aspera* of the Romans.

Cold asperity may reign on the heights, but down in the valley, sheltered by the great, white Canigou, a delicious winter climate brings out almond flower and mimosa in February, and on Carnival days, so warm that one seeks shade under still leafless trees, one sees couples bunching together in the Bail de la Courre, and on a long-drawn-out note the girls jumping into the air aided by the men. They shoot up above the heads of the watching crowd to kiss each other in mid-air. This dance seems to be derived from the Volta * which came into Provence from Italy, and into Roussillon from Provence. Here it is Lo Salt, the Jump, and is done also by one couple alone when the girl appears for a moment sitting on her partner's hand. This lifting of the woman is a feature of Catalan dancing on both sides of the frontier. After the Bail de la Posta the girls ride off on their partners' shoulders, as also in

* See *Dances of France*, vol. II, in this series.

the local Quadrille, and custom requires the bridegroom's nearest male relative thus to carry the bride to the bridal chamber on the eve of her wedding—but this points to an ancient 'first right' far removed from Lo Salt.

DANCES INNUMERABLE

Up at Mont-Louis there is a little Baillet for one couple at a time, and down on the coast a variant called Bail dels Rosers. Rosers are girls who devote themselves to church duties, yet arrange village balls and process with their own Virgin on festival days. Roussillon abounds in these sororities and fraternities. The woman's steps in Pair dances are low and discreet, her skirts held by finger and thumb well in front. The man often raises his arms, Jota fashion, but uses neither finger clicks nor castanets. The delicate, graceful waving of the men's arms so characteristic of Spanish Catalonia * is lacking here.

Various ceremonies are carried out most seriously. On festal occasions we see the *ramelets* (sprigs), when each young man buys a bouquet of horrible artificial flowers—with fresh mimosa and camellias to be had for the taking—to present with sugared almonds to his partner. But the dance itself may be anything, a Gallop, a Valse or a Two-Step. The Bail dels Coumfits (sweets) has a similar opening, in fact any dance may be thus inaugurated. There is also a more homely amusement, the Bail de l'Ascoumbe, the Broom dance. This begins with a Gallop, or a sedate walk, men's arms round their partners' waists. There must be an extra girl. One man dances with a broom, gives it to a girl, runs from her to another. The one left then dances with the broom, a man comes to dance with her, she leaves the broom on the floor before the deserted girl, and so on interminably. The tune is the charming Bepa ballad. And of course there is the Sardana.

* For Catalan dances see *Dances of Spain*, vol. II, in this series.

FARANDOLE AND CONTRAPÁS

Chain dances seem to be indigenous since Iberian days, for we see on Iberian pottery found at Liria a fourth-century B.C. chain dancing to the music of a double pipe. They are called Catalan Farandole and Bal Infernal; one is done to the sinister Carmagnole of revolutionary memory—

> *Baillarem la Farandola*
> *En despit de Charles Dou.*

Dou means 'ten', and the verse sounds as though the Bourbon restoration was not popular in this corner of France.

The strange old Contrapás, itself a Chain, has only just died out. It was performed after mass to a doleful *divino*, in which the dancers antiphonally declared themselves miserable sinners; it was sometimes led by the parish priest and afterwards by Cap and Cua, Head and Tail men, who knew the words of the long litany and led the dance.

CARNIVAL

Ceremonial Carnival dances are the Cascabaillada at the little watering-place Amélie-les-Bains, its variant the Entrallissada, at Arles-sur-Tech, and the Encadenat at Prats-de-Mollo, all processionals through narrow Pyrenean streets. In old days men sprinkled their partners with scent from beautifully shaped *almoratxas*, which charming custom still lives on the other side of the frontier. On the French side they now pass a Catalan jug of wine as a loving-cup. On Carnival Monday night we see the long, white line of the Tious-tious, all clad in their wives' best chemises and nightcaps, bent forward at a swaying trot, each trying to light the paper tail of the man in front. A special tune accompanies this exercise, old as the hills around.

Up at Prats-de-Mollo on Carnival Monday there is a

mock bullfight with agile cows, Sardanas swinging all over the *place* until interrupted by a nimble cow, her horns tied up with ribbons. When she has disappeared full tilt down the street, the Gentleman and the Lady (who is the traditional Man-woman) marshal a long procession headed by a red-barretina'd man bearing the post. This *posta* is painted with lilies and a simpering girl's face on one side, a leering devil's face on the other. Now begins the extraordinary Bail de la Posta, a public test of a girl's virtue, a sort of trial by ordeal. Up come the dancers in pairs or in threes, a man with a girl on either side. If a girl is well-behaved the side showing the lilies of innocence is presented and kissed by her; if her character is doubtful the *posta* is reversed and she is made to salute the devil. She then coolly turns about to receive a slap behind with the *posta*. The crowd gives its advice and has been heard to call 'Hit her hard!' An amazing sight it is to see dozens of girls in spotless Catalan caps or modern Carnival dress, butterflies and fairies, calmly submitting to this public walloping. They then ride off on their partners' shoulders. The *posta* is put up to auction the Sunday before and the man who bids highest obtains the honour of wielding it.

THE BEAR HUNT

This is one of those strange survivals of an ancient animal-divinity, caught, married, killed and mourned. The chief dance is performed by the 'trainer', for the Pyrenean dancing bear is inevitably confused with his long-ago wild ancestor. The trainer dances beautifully before his beast, shaving him, and catching soap, basin and towel, which come hurtling over the heads of the crowd in the dance. This wonderful persistence of an antique rite is found in several Catalan villages, in Andorra, and in the Central Pyrenees. At Arles-sur-Tech it is carried out with great care and zest.

Plate 2   *La Castagne. Balaguères*

THE LEZ VALLEY AND BALAGUÈRES

We leave Mediterranean culture, flora and scenery. The ethnological type changes. These valleys, high in the mountains of Ariège, already on the Atlantic watershed, speak a western form of the *langue d'oc*, show a western form of dance and a fine mixture of eastern and western song. Revived dances and re-made costumes have been alive for twenty years and more, and both are saved for at least another generation.

On festal days young men carry a *ramelet* from door to door, not now a sprig as it should be, but an orange on a plate. This used to be larded over with *louis-d'or* but now humbly rests on three coins stuck into it like three legs. Another man carries a mass of tiny bouquets of wild flowers—the real *ramelet*—and the pair dance Bourrée steps before the householder who contributes to the fête and receives a bouquet. Sometimes a covered cake is suddenly displayed on receiving a coin. But it is only to admire. It is the dancers who eat it after the ball.

Amongst dances of this region is La Traversée, a Country dance form for two couples *vis-à-vis*. There are variants at the head of the Lez valley, at Sentein for instance, where it is danced by six. Here, in the butcher's kitchen under the joints and hams hanging from the beams, we spent a memorable evening, warmth within, snow outside. The Traversée was danced to a Bepa variant, far from the home of that Catalan ballad. The best dances are the Bourrée—for there are many Bourrées throughout France in spite of the shocked surprise of the people of Auvergne who consider it their monopoly—and the Castagne (the Chestnut), which may follow or may be danced separately. Both are exceedingly gay and the first exceedingly tiring. A charming old-fashioned Valse is danced, a Polka Piqué, and the usual cast-off ballroom dances—Schottische, Quadrille and so on —now become 'folk' dances.

THE VALLEY OF CAMPAN

The old province of Bigorre, now included in the department of Hautes-Pyrénées, has two main valleys. That of Campan leads up to the great Tourmalet pass, the other, opening at Lourdes, ends beneath the snowy Cirque de Gavarnie. This valley is full of men's seasonal dances, but it is in Campan that the best recreational dances are found. They were taught to the founder of the present group of dancers when she was a girl of thirteen by a very old man and represent the real dances of the 'pays' in use two generations before Mazurka, Schottische and Polka had come to the countryfolk—which were all the girl's own parents knew. A fête may open with a Passe-Carrère, literally 'passing through the street'; this is used for weddings also, led by the best dancer or the groomsman who picks up his string of followers by thudding his wand of office on the ground in front of them. A gay, leaping step belongs to 'Mai, Mai' (Mother, Mother, marry me now); a local Branle begins with a ring, to end with ribbons crossed on the ground and steps across them; a Ribbon or Sash dance is done by men and girls, but should, I think, be a men's dance, for in the next valley it belongs to the ritual Balladins who come out in the spring.

WITCHES' DANCES

An exceedingly interesting, not to say sinister, flavour is given to some of these dances, for the old man who divulged them solemnly declared they belonged to the local witches whom he had seen performing them 'in a copse' high on the side of the great Pic du Midi de Bigorre. Yet they belong to ordinary folk as well—which is in keeping with our knowledge of the witch cult, for whatever dances were done in the region were used by witches and warlocks at their gatherings. There was always a follow-my-leader dance, which is a Farandole—and always a ring. The Pelha ded Gat (the Cat's Skin) is however unique, and by its name, so closely connected with witches, and its queer, squatting postures, really seems to invoke the ecstatic moment when the ritualists sought to transform themselves into animal form—and probably thought they succeeded. The end of the dance is now a competition as to who can keep up the squatting Kibby, or Cossack, step the longest.

THE BASQUE COUNTRY

Travelling westwards we pass through the old kingdom of Béarn, famous for scarlet *capulets* and the ancient Branle, to find another people and another tongue where Béarn meets La Soule, the first of the Basque provinces. These much-discussed people belong to a race, probably autochthonous, already occupying the region when the Indo-European waves came in on their rising tide. They have no affinities with the Gallo-Roman and Spanish peoples around them and have always been spoken of as something apart. A Basque type, or rather two or three Basque types are very noticeable, those on the northern slope of the Pyrenees being easily recognisable amongst the French (Gascon) population touching them. Those on the southern side, of another type, can equally easily be recognised amongst the intruding Spanish population.

The Basque language has been under scientific investigation for the last hundred years. Like the people who speak it, it is pre-Indo-European and was long considered a descendant of the lost Iberian tongue. Quite other theses are now being worked upon, but one thing is certain: it is not a 'mixture of French and Spanish', as tourists still blithely announce. The Basques may be dark or fair, have blue eyes or brown, but their chief characteristic is agility. Their walk is superb, their ball game amazing and their dancing amazing too.

Although they are such famous dancers, no Basque dances have been selected for notation here, for they are almost entirely men's dances for ceremonial use. Women appear in two only, and one of these has already been dealt with in its liveliest form as the Aragonese Jota.* On the French side it is called Fandango and has changed its character considerably, becoming languid on the coast, and is danced with finger and thumb clicks without castanets. On the Spanish-Basque side it is Jota again in name, and its relationship is more clearly seen.

The other dance in which women may take part is Dantza Khorda (the String Dance) on the French side, Auresku on the Spanish side. Here it is ornate, the leader's partner fetched from her house by four men, showers of tricky steps danced before her until she is presented with a handkerchief-end and led into the 'string'. Dantza Khorda is simpler, but leader and last man carry bouquets.

Other famous dances are the Saut Basque, called Mutil Dantza (the Young Men's Dance) on the Spanish side, and the Sword dances of the Spanish Basques. That from Berriz, Biscay, has been brought across the frontier and is danced indiscriminately everywhere, much to the detriment of true regional tradition. This transplanted, virile dance is belittled by being taught to young boys and even to girls—a ridiculous sight. The Carnival masquerades of La Soule are amazing in dance and drama, but are of too anthropological a character to describe here. Their chief dances are the Wine-glass Dance of the famous Hobby Horse, a dance still called Gavotte, to the tune of Vestris' stage Gavotte, and the March of the Masquerades composed of the classical ballet Pas de Basque. Entrechats dix seem child's play to these young villagers, together with many other ballet steps.

Local instruments are the six-stringed drum already described,† called *ttun-ttun* by onomatopoeia, and the *tchirula*,

* See *Dances of Spain*, vol. II. † *Ib.*, p. 15.

a three-holed pipe. On the Spanish side we hear the *txistu* and small drum played by one man or by an ensemble of three or more. These peculiarly Spanish-Basque instruments have, like the Sword dance, flooded over the frontier and are helping to confuse regional tradition beyond repair.

MUSIC

Roussillon. Here is heard the Cobla band at every festivity. A well-known band is that of Céret. It is engaged all night and most of the next day during the last days of Carnival, and its *Cap* or chief knows custom, procedure and traditional airs better than the people who engage him. The band consists of the strident prime and tenor (woodwind instruments peculiar to both the Catalonias), a cornet à pistons, a brass bass and a string double-bass. This odd ensemble produces a unique and exciting sound. The shrill *flaviol* and tiny drum are added to the mixture on the Spanish side.

When young men go Pace-egging (as we should say) at Easter, they sing Goigs dels Oùs (Joys of the Eggs). One example from Mont-Louis consists of but four bars of song, followed by an eight-bar refrain played on a small flageolet:

GOIGS DEL OÙS

Noted by Violet Alford at Mont-Louis

Bin-giu oùs à la cin - tel - la, al sept goigs sont a - gue bats.

Refrain on pipe

Shepherds on the Canigou go Pace-egging to the high farms

with a *gratlle*, a home-made six-holed pipe of boxwood. Every feast has its tunes; even the mules on the day of their ceremonial blessing have theirs, without which 'they will not trot'. The Gavotte air of the famous Vestris has somehow got into the repertory of Pyrenean musicians; the whole range knows also the Bear tune, which in the west becomes the Wineglass dance of the Basque Hobby Horse; the Matelote, which we know as Rigs of Marlow in England and Rakes of Mallow in Ireland, begins in Provence and finishes on the Atlantic shore; a delightful Noël noted at Prats-de-Mollo—

> *Salten i ballen las pastorets dones,*
> *Salten i ballen la Nit de Nadal*

—becomes part of a Spanish-Basque Sword-dance tune; the tragic Catalan ballad La Bepa becomes a Countrydance air in Ariège. So although each great region has its characteristics, the whole remains Pyrenean.

The Lez Valley and Balaguères. Dance tunes are not remarkable but there is a wealth of folk song drawn from east and west. One of the loveliest is L'Agnel, and a good version of the Pyrenean song Aqueres Mountagnos was sung to me here. This air, long used as Toulouse Radio signal, is said to have been composed by Gaston Phoebus, Comte de Foix. The only instrument peculiar to the valley is a rustic oboe played by an old shepherd who accompanies the dancers. Bourrée and Castagne are wood-wind tunes.

Campan. Here we meet the antique Pyrenean six-stringed drum (see Plate 1) and the three-holed pipe played by the same musician, which is found also in Upper Aragon and in Béarn although the Basques claim it as their own. Dance tunes show a strong likeness to those of the next Bigorre valley. At St-Savin we find Balladins, ritual dancing men, who have preserved the tunes in better shape than at Campan. Eras Abricoutets (Apricots) for instance is a lovely tune there and a poor one at Campan.

The Vallée d'Ossau is 'the country where they sing', as indeed is the whole of Béarn. Here traditional song reaches its apogee in a thousand beautiful modal love songs. There are many examples of the Night Visit Song

Tu frapperas à la fenestro,

and a cycle of Chansons de Neuf. These spring from some numerical magic. 'Under my foot there are nine jonquils' and 'I bring nine apples', nine roses or nine pink piglets. The famous Branles of the Ossau valley are accompanied by the Pyrenean stringed drum and three-holed pipe.

COSTUME

Roussillon. The scarlet stocking cap or *barretina* has travelled up the length of Italy and round the Gulf of Lions, and on fête days is worn with a scarlet or dark sash and elaborate espadrilles laced high up the leg. White shirt and trousers complete the men's holiday dress. The woman's costume is a modern dress (and appears to have been so for many years), with the Catalan cap and a Paisley-patterned shawl of finest wool, a silk apron often black, and embroidered, laced-up espadrilles. The cap is made in four parts: a full black silk cap, a black silk head-band, a beautifully fine white lace cap over the black one, and a white lace strip over the black band. The whole is drawn up to fit the head and worn towards the back, so that the hair shows in front. At the top of the Tet valley a black head-kerchief replaces this cap.

Balaguères. This costume is typically Pyrenean, men and women wearing hand-woven striped woollen stuff, chiefly in greys and blues. The women wear large aprons striped, flowered or plain, sunbonnet-like white caps, and shoulder shawls beautifully patterned. The men are gay with scarlet *barretina*, as in Roussillon, red sash, a gaudy waistcoat, and woollen pompons to finish a wool tie; the striped coat has plain sleeves. Men and women wear embroidered espadrilles and in bad weather enormously turned-up sabots. In the Bethmale valley the points soar nearly to the knees. Young men make these for their sweethearts, and the more they admire them the higher go the points.

Campan. Here we come upon the famous scarlet *capulet* supposed to belong only to the Béarnais valley of Ossau. In Campan it is of the same fine cloth, but is edged with black velvet instead of being turned back with rose-coloured brocade as in Ossau. Otherwise the dress is more akin to that of Balaguères, the home-woven skirt is brilliantly striped, heavily pleated round the waist; the white cap worn beneath the *capulet* is lightly hand-quilted, of cotton with embroidery. The apron often has beautifully vandyked cuttings round its fitting waistpiece and is tied with a woollen cord. Its pockets are embroidered and appliqué'd with coloured cloth flowers; the sleeveless corsage, slightly basqued, is lined with violet and green material.

The men wear dark trousers and hand-knitted short coats, purplish-blue or brown, with wavy lines and flowers embroidered on the knitting. Under the collar goes a woollen cord ending in tassels or pompons. The béret is very large and held out flat as a plate by a twist of rushes inside. Espadrilled feet slip into upturned sabots. Both men and women, being keepers of sheep, wear salt pockets round their waists embroidered with names, flowers or hearts.

Widows wear a *capuchon* of black, lined with scarlet, reaching to the hem of the dress—an imposing sight. Instead of the basket carried on the back by Alpine people these Pyreneans carry an oblong bag about 2 ft. in length provided with two straps of the same material to pass over the shoulders. When made of their bright striped stuffs it is a gay affair and far less cumbersome than the Swiss basket.

FESTIVALS AND SEASONS
WHEN DANCING MAY BE SEEN

Candlemas (*February 2nd*) — Bear Hunt rites in Vallespir.

Carnival — In some places opens on January 1st. Chief days are the Thursday, Sunday, Monday and Tuesday before Lent. Amazing doings in Vallespir, ritual Balladins in Bigorre, Bear Hunt at Gèdre and Luz, men's dances in the Basque Country.

Ash Wednesday — The Death of Carnival everywhere, especially ornate at Amélie-les-Bains.

Easter — Goigs dels Oùs (Pace-egging) in Roussillon. Modern fêtes at tourist centres must not be confused with traditional festivals.

Whitsuntide — Pilgrimage to Our Lady of the Hawthorns above Ainhoa; fête near by.

May — Wool fair at Castillon-en-Couserans when costumes may be seen. Maypoles in villages of the foothills, especially in Gascony.

Trinity Sunday — Procession des Cavaliers (Saracens and Christians) at Martres-Tolosane.

Corpus Christi (*Fête-Dieu*) — Dancing processions in Basse-Navarre on the Sunday after Corpus Christi and its octave.

Midsummer Eve — Bonfires, torches; *brandons* (whole trees) in the Luchon and Bagnères regions; dancing round them everywhere.

St. Aloysius (*June 25th*)	Blessing of the mules and other animals in Roussillon and elsewhere.
Feast of the Assumption (*August 15th*)	Village patronal fêtes abound on this date. Dancing will go on all night. Zezensusko (Fire Bull) in Basque villages. The fête at Laruns, Val d'Ossau, is famous for its costumes and Branles.
October 7th	Fête at St-Bertrand-de-Comminges.
Christmas	Wassailing songs; also at New Year and on St. Agatha's Day (February 5th), especially in the Basque Country.

SOME GROUPS OF REGIONAL DANCERS

Foment de la Sardana, Perpignan, Pyrénées-Orientales.

Les Danseurs et Chanteurs de Balaguères. The leaders are to be found at Castillon-en-Couserans, Ariège.

Les Pastourelles de Campan, Hautes-Pyrénées.

Les Troubadours de Comminges, St-Gaudens, Haute-Garonne.

Groups of dancers now exist in many places. They are not always trustworthy guardians of their traditions. In Bigorre traditional, seasonal dancing men should be seen. In the Basque Country modern groups swamp traditional village dancers, annexing the fêtes and the dancing places. They show invented dances for girls, fancy costumes instead of traditional Basque dress, Spanish-Basque dances and instruments in France. They should be ignored but there is often nothing else to be seen. One of the finest dance traditions in Europe is rapidly disappearing through these causes.

THE DANCES

TECHNICAL EDITORS
MURIEL WEBSTER AND KATHLEEN P. TUCK

ABBREVIATIONS
USED IN DESCRIPTION OF STEPS AND DANCES

r—right ⎱ referring to R—right ⎱ describing turns or
l—left ⎰ hand, foot, etc. L—left ⎰ ground pattern
C—clockwise C-C—counter-clockwise

For descriptions of foot positions and explanations of any ballet terms the following books are suggested for reference:

A Primer of Classical Ballet (Cecchetti method). Cyril Beaumont.

First Steps (R.A.D.). Ruth French and Felix Demery.

The Ballet Lover's Pocket Book. Kay Ambrose.

Reference books for description of figures:

The Scottish Country Dance Society's Publications. Many volumes, from Thornhill, Cairnmuir Road, Edinburgh 12.

The English Folk Dance and Song Society's Publications. Cecil Sharp House, 2 Regent's Park Road, London N.W.1.

The Country Dance Book I–VI. Cecil J. Sharp. Novello & Co., London.

POISE OF THE BODY AND HOLDS

The men are lithe and light, the women less so. No directions can be given to cover all regions, for there is much variety: in Roussillon the girls are free and debonair, in the Central Pyrenees more discreet. When dancing backwards, as in the Bourrée Ariégeoise, the men often bend forward considerably, drawing their partners after them, who then lean back. Espadrilles allow a remarkable lightness.

Arm movements are not prescribed except the Jota-like raising of the arms with flexed elbows each side of the head, hands at head level, in Balaguères dances.

BASIC STEPS

There are no really basic steps except the classical ballet steps found as folk steps all along the Pyrenees.

	Beats
1. *Encadenat*	
Step forward on r foot.	1
Hop on r foot, beating l foot behind r calf. (Pas battu.)	and
Repeat, beginning on l foot.	2 and
N.B.—Two pas battus to a bar.	
2. *Bourrée Step*	
Spring on to r foot.	1
Again on to r foot.	2
Change l, r.	1 and
Hop on l foot.	2
This is repeated throughout the dance (always springing on to the r foot), the whole step taking two bars. The men fling out the l leg in an elegant battement while springing on to r foot; or turn the spring into a pas battu,	

or any other ornamentations. The girls perform the step low on the ground.

3. *La Castagne*

The man improvises any step he chooses, his partner following. They often begin with this step:—

Step on r foot, passing l foot across r ankle.	1
Hop on r foot, tapping l toe on ground.	2
Step on l foot, passing r foot across l ankle.	1
Hop on l foot, tapping r toe on ground.	2

BAIL DE LA COURRE

Region   General in Roussillon. Plate 3.

Character   Very lively, even romping for Gallop, agile and light for lifts.

Formation   First a couple dance, then in groups.

Dance

FIGURE I

Couples gallop round dancing-place, ordinary Valse hold. Occasionally the man may turn his partner under his l arm in front of him. The last 8 bars are sung in each repeat. Repeat all if desired.	MUSIC *Bars* 1–16 repeated last
End in groups of 2, 3 or 4 couples forming small circles and facing inwards.	time: 8–14
A long-drawn-out note on cornet (as indicated in music). Music now follows dancers—*rallentando* if there is delay in forming groups.	(15–16: *rall.* & pause)

FIGURE II

Women put their hands on the shoulders of the men. Men put their hands under the women's arms. | 1–4

Women jump to help men to lift them as high as possible (see sketch). | 5–6

Women lean inward and kiss each other in the air. They descend slowly, helped by the men. | 7–8

Gallop in couples as in Fig. I, but for 24 bars, the last 8 of which are sung. | 9–16
| 1–16

Repeat the whole dance five or six times.

On the last three bars the last time through, the woman prepares to spring on to her partner's r shoulder. She turns her back to him, standing close, and springs, he helping her with a hand under either arm and a strong lift. The man then carries her away.

LO SALT (THE JUMP)

Instead of joining a group, a single couple may perform Lo Salt. The woman places her l hand in the man's r (he turning towards her) and her r hand on his l shoulder. At the same time he places his l hand under her r | 1–6
| or
| *ad lib*.

26

BAIL DE LA COURRE

Noted by Violet Alford at Arles-sur-Tech
Arranged by Arnold Foster

BAIL DE LA COURRE
(Another tune to alternate with the first)

Noted by Violet Alford at Prats-de-Mollo
Arranged by Arnold Foster

arm. She leaps as high as possible, he rapidly slides his l hand down her side and opens it wide, palm upward. She sits for a second on his hand, shoulder-high, and descends gently. (Other ways of performing this feat are quite permissible.)

7–8

During the dance some of the men spray the women with scent from *almoratxas* tied with ribbons. Those carrying the *almoratxas* will not be able to take part in the lift. A characteristic *almoratxa* is shown in Plate 3.

Plate 3   Bail de la Courre: Lo Salt. Roussillon

ENCADENAT

(Linked Dance)

Region   Prats-de-Mollo, Vallespir, at Carnival only.

Character   Processional, light and lively.

Formation   Any number of couples behind one another, woman on R of man. The arms hang loosely by the sides. All face up, partners standing about 4 ft. apart. Before beginning the dance a Catalan jug of wine is passed as a loving-cup.

Dance	MUSIC Bars
Men move forward diagonally to R, women move forward diagonally to L. Man crosses in front of his partner, thus changing places and moving about 6 ft. farther on. All use these steps:—	
4 pas battus (see Basic Steps No. 1). Two steps to each bar of music.	1–2
One complete turn; feet together or pirouette.	3–4
4 pas battus.	5–6
One complete turn.	7–8
A leisurely assemblé (feet together) and adjust places.	9–10
Repeat movements of bars 1–10 as often as necessary during procession down the street. The diagonal crossing is continued throughout.	11–20

ENCADENAT
Cascabaillada tune

Noted by Violet Alford
and Sibella Bonham-Carter
Arranged by Arnold Foster

BOURRÉE ARIÉGEOISE

Region   Ariège, especially Lez Valley and Balaguères.

Character   Very gay, agile and quick.

Formation   For any number of couples standing round in a circle.

Dance	MUSIC
Step: Bourrée step (see Basic Steps No. 2) throughout.	Bars
INTRODUCTION. Couples stand still, facing centre, all holding hands in a circle.	(4 bars or more)
1 Still holding hands in a ring, dancers move in circle C, men often turning towards their partners and dancing backwards. The men embellish the steps with grands battements, brisés, pas battus, and other fancies.	1–16
2 Women dance once round their partners in a wide circle; men dance on the spot. All have arms raised with bent elbows, hand at head level.	1–16
3 Repeat ring C, as in 1.	1–16
4 Men dance in wide circle round their partners, women dance on the spot. Arms as in 2.	1–16
5 Ring C as in 1.	1–16
6 Couples link r arms and turn, still using Bourrée step.	1–8
Couples link l arms and turn.	9–16
7 Ring C as in 1.	1–16

BOURRÉE ARIÉGEOISE

Noted by Violet Alford
Arranged by Arnold Foster

8 Men turn women continuously under their r arms.	1–16
9 Ring C as in 1.	1–16
10 Women dance in front of their own partners and behind the next man, continuing thus, alternately in front and behind the men,	1–16

once round the ring to places. Arms are
held raised as in 2. Men dance on the spot.

11 Ring C as in 1.   1–16

This dance is followed immediately by La Castagne.

LA CASTAGNE (*The Chestnut*)

Region   As for Bourrée Ariégeoise. Plate 2.

Character   Gay, quick and showy.

Formation   The circle formation is kept ; the best couple go into the centre, the rest squat, the women's skirts spread round them. All clap throughout, marking the value of each note, not merely each beat.

Dance   MUSIC
The dancing couple may begin with the step described in Basic Steps (No. 3). If not, the man sets any step he likes, which his partner must copy. Each step is repeated throughout the value of 8 or 16 bars of music.   *Bars*

1 Man holds woman by both hands and swings her rapidly C.   (8 or 16)

2 Woman dances once round man, arms raised as in Bourrée.   (8)
Man dances once round woman, arms raised.   (8)

3 Couple turn *vis-à-vis* to perform Piqué or other steps on the spot.   (8 or 16)

LA CASTAGNE

Quick and gay

Noted by Violet Alford
Arranged by Arnold Foster

4 Couple link r arms and turn rapidly C.   (8 or 16)
  Couple link l arms to repeat rapid turn C-C.

5 Man turns woman rapidly under his r arm,   (8 or 16)
  always in the same direction. (Her skirts
  billow out like a balloon.)

ERA PELHA DED GAT

(*The Cat's Skin*)

Region The two main valleys of Bigorre, Hautes Pyrénées. Plates 1 and 4.

Character A strange dance entirely in a squatting position, said to be a witches' dance. Nowadays it ends with an almost frenzied competition in the Kibby or Cossack step.

Formation Any number of couples, partners *vis-à-vis* round a circle or in a longways formation. The women tuck their voluminous skirts between their knees, pulling the back fullness through to the front. All squat.

Dance

	MUSIC Bars
1 The man gives both hands to his partner and turns her once round C in a series of little jumps, two to a bar, both squatting.	A 1–8
Repeat C-C.	1–8

ERA PELHA DED GAT

From Campan. Noted by Violet Alford
Arranged by Arnold Foster

2	Let go hands. Each dancer turns C-C singly, 8 little jumps, still squatting. Repeat, turning C-C.	B 9-12 13-16
3	The man turns his partner under his r arm, both jumping in the squatting position. The woman turns the man under her l arm, jumping as in bars 1-4.	A 1-4 5-8
4	The men jump into the centre and give both hands to another man and turn each other once. Meanwhile the women turn their backs to the centre and begin to jump away squatting.	B 9-16 A 1-8
5	The men drop hands and perform the Kibby step singly for as long as they can; the women, still squatting, jump out of the dancing-place.	A & B *ad lib.*

[The last time I saw this dance, each man gave both hands to his partner and both together performed the Kibby step as long as they could. As each individual tired he or she let go hands, rose and walked away. Those left continued singly, moving about all over the dancing-space as they performed. The lookers-on and the other dancers rushed to their favourite performers and stood over them clapping, shouting and throwing in bérets and handkerchiefs to encourage them. The strongest may endure for two or three repeats of the music.

The older manner was far more in keeping with the name and tradition of a witches' dance and it gave a sinister impression. The competition of endurance then took quite a secondary place.]

Plate 4   Vallée de Campan

BIBLIOGRAPHY

ALFORD, VIOLET.—*Pyrenean Festivals*. London, 1937.
—— 'The Basque Masquerade.' *Folk-Lore*, vol. XXXIX, 1928.
—— 'The Springtime Bear in the Pyrenees.' *Folk-Lore*, vol. XLI, 1930.
—— 'Dance and Song in Two Pyrenean Valleys.' *The Musical Quarterly*, New York, April 1931.
—— 'Ceremonial Dances of the Spanish Basques.' *The Musical Quarterly*, July 1932.
—— 'The Farandole.' *The Dancing Times*, June 1933.
—— 'Some Notes on the Pyrenean Stringed Drum.' *Revue Internationale des Etudes Basques*, Sept. 1935.
—— ' Traditional Airs from a Little-Known Pyrenean Valley.' *The Musical Quarterly*, July 1939.

(All the above contain music and illustrations.)

AZKUE, RESURRECCIÓN MARIA DE.—*Cancionero Popular Vasco*, vols. III and IV: *Danzas*. Barcelona, [1920].
COLLIER, BASIL.—*Catalan France*. London, 1939.
DONOSTIA, JOSÉ ANTONIO DE.—*Euskel Eres-Sorta*. 1921. (Basque folk tunes.)
GALLOP, RODNEY.—*A Book of the Basques*. London, 1930. (Airs and illustrations.)
HÉRELLE, GEORGES.—*Le Théâtre comique*. (*Etudes sur le théâtre basque.*) Paris, 1925–26.
POUEIGH, JEAN.—*Chansons populaires des Pyrénées françaises*. Paris, 1926.
VIDAL, PIERRE.—*Goigs dels Oùs*. Perpignan, 1888. (Notes and songs of Pace-egging.)

Note.—There are no dance books on Pyrenean dances.